Collins

easy learning

Phonics

Ages 4–5

shoe

Carol Medcalf

How to use this book

This book is designed to help your child be better prepared for starting school and assist them during their reception year to back up learning in school. It follows the recommended phonics system and order used in most reception classes. Activities increase in difficulty as your child works through the book to challenge and extend their knowledge and skills.

- Find a quiet, comfortable place to work, away from distractions.

- This book has been written in a logical order, so start at the first page and work your way through.

- Help with reading the instructions where necessary and ensure that your child understands what to do.

- This book is a gentle introduction to 37 of the 44 sounds of the English language. Working through the book, your child will start to realise that words are made up of small separate sounds. These individual sounds are called phonemes; bus, for example, is made up of three phonemes: b-u-s. Encourage your child to sound out each letter sound before they attempt to read the whole word. For example, say 'kuh-a-tuh' and then read 'cat'. Some sounds are represented by two letters (digraph), such as sh. For these sounds your child should sound out the single sh sound and not the individual letter sounds. Where this occurs the sounds have always been underlined to emphasise they make one sound.

- If an activity is too difficult for your child then do more of our suggested practical activities (see Activity note) and return to the page when you know that they're likely to achieve it.

- Always end each activity before your child gets tired so that they will be eager to return next time.

- Help and encourage your child to check their own answers as they complete each activity.

- Let your child return to their favourite pages once they have been completed. Talk about the activities they enjoyed and what they have learnt.

Special features of this book:

- **Activity note:** situated at the bottom of every left-hand page, this suggests further activities and encourages discussion about what your child has learnt.

- **Progress panel:** situated at the bottom of every right-hand page, the number of animals and stars shows your child how far they have progressed through the book. Once they have completed each double page, ask them to colour in the white star.

- **Certificate:** the certificate on page 24 should be used to reward your child for their effort and achievement. Remember to give them plenty of praise and encouragement, regardless of how they do.

Published by Collins
An imprint of HarperCollins*Publishers* Ltd
The News Building
1 London Bridge Street
London
SE1 9GF

Browse the complete Collins catalogue at
www.collins.co.uk

© HarperCollins*Publishers* Ltd 2013
This edition © HarperCollins*Publishers* Ltd 2015

10 9 8 7

ISBN 978-0-00-815164-5

The author asserts the moral right to be identified as the author of this work.

All rights reserved. No part of this publication may be reproduced, stored in a retrieval system, or transmitted, in any form or by any means, electronic, mechanical, photocopying, recording or otherwise, without the prior permission of Collins.

British Library Cataloguing in Publication Data

A Catalogue record for this publication is available from the British Library.

Written by Carol Medcalf
Page layout by Linda Miles, Lodestone Publishing and Contentra Technologies Ltd
Illustrated by Jenny Tulip
Cover design by Sarah Duxbury and Paul Oates
Cover illustration by John Haslam
Project managed by Chantal Peacock and Sonia Dawkins

Contents

Phonic sounds s, a, t and p

● Say the word for each picture. Draw a circle round the letter sound it starts with.

s   a   t   p

s   a   t   p

s   a   t   p

s   a   t   p

● Say the word for each picture. Write the letter sound it starts with.

S

Phonic sounds i, n, m and d

● Say the word for each picture. Draw a circle round the letter sound it starts with.

i	n	m	d
i	n	m	d
i	n	m	d
i	n	m	d

● Say the word for each picture. Write the letter sound it starts with.

☐   ☐

Well done!
Now colour
the star.

Practice time!

● Look at the letter in each set. Draw a circle round the pictures that start with the letter sound.

Reading with phonics

- Say the sounds you have learnt so far, **s**, **a**, **t**, **p**, **i**, **n**, **m**, and **d**. Use the sounds to spell out these words. Sound out each letter.

is   it   in   at

- Say the words for the pictures below. Draw lines to match the words to the pictures.

sad   man   pin   tap

Well done! Now colour the next star.

7

Phonic sounds g, o, c and k

● Say the word for each picture. Draw a ⬭circle round the letter sound it starts with.

g   o   c   k

g   o   c   k

g   o   c   k

g   o   c   k

● Say the word for each picture. Write the letter sound it starts with.

Phonic sounds <u>ck</u>, e, u and r

● Say the words for these pictures. Some make the <u>ck</u> sound at the end. Join the ones that make the <u>ck</u> sound to the big blue <u>ck</u>.

ck

● Say the word for each picture. Draw a circle round the letter sound it starts with.

r
e
u

r
u
e

r
u
e

r
u
e

e
u
r

Practice time!

- Look at the letter in each set. Draw a circle round the pictures that start with the letter sound.

Play voice games together. Say: 'Can you make your voice go down a slide? Wheeeeee. Hiss like a snake, hissss. Talk quietly and say shhhhh. Sound surprised and say oooooooo.' This will help your child to pronounce letter sounds.

More reading with phonics

● Try reading these words by sounding out each letter. Draw lines to match the words to the pictures.

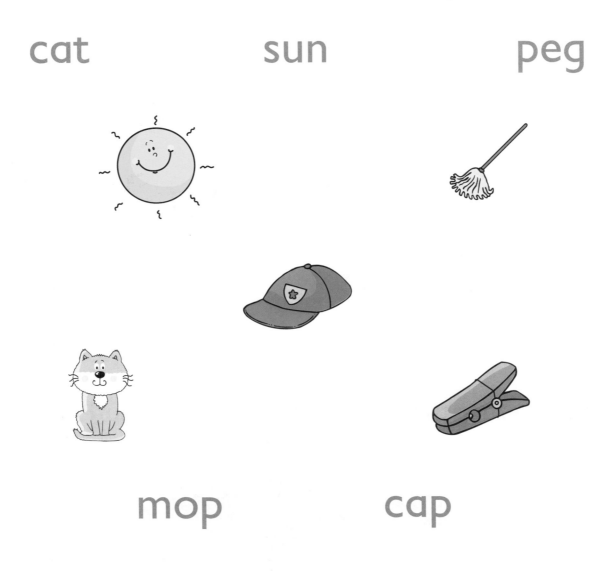

cat   sun   peg

mop   cap

● Now try reading these words.

him   run   pat

Phonic sounds h, b, f and <u>ff</u>

- Look at the letter at the start of each row. Cross out the picture that does **not** start with the same letter sound.

h

b

f

- Say together the long **<u>ff</u>** sound heard in hu**<u>ff</u>** and pu**<u>ff</u>**. Circle the **ff** sounds around the Billy Goats Gru**<u>ff</u>**.

Talk about the <u>ff</u>, <u>ll</u>, and <u>ss</u> sounds, found at the end of words. With your child, think of some more words ending in these double letters e.g. fluff, cliff, pull, tall, pass, kiss.

Phonic sounds l, ll and ss

● Say the words for the pictures. Join the dots to write the letter l to finish the words.

l eaf

l adybird

l ion

l adder

● Say the words for these pictures.

Hear the long **ll** and **ss** sounds.

● Circle the pictures that have the **ll** or **ss** sound.

ll

ss

Well done! Now colour the next star.

Phonic sounds j, v, w and x

● Say the word for each picture. Draw a circle round the letter sound it starts with.

	j	v	w	x
(windmill)	j	v	w	x
(jelly)	j	v	w	x
(van)	j	v	w	x
(x-ray)	j	v	w	x
(violin)	j	v	w	x
(jam)	j	v	w	x

● Say the word for each picture. Write the letter sound it starts with.

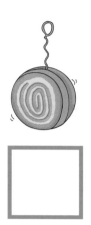

☐ ☐

● Say the sound zz and qu. Write zz or qu to finish the words.

pi __ __ a

__ __ een

__ __ arter

pu __ __ le

Well done!
Now colour
the next star.

Real words and silly words

- Using the sounds you know, read these words. Circle the real words.

ip   on   ug   if

- Read these words. Draw a picture to match the words.

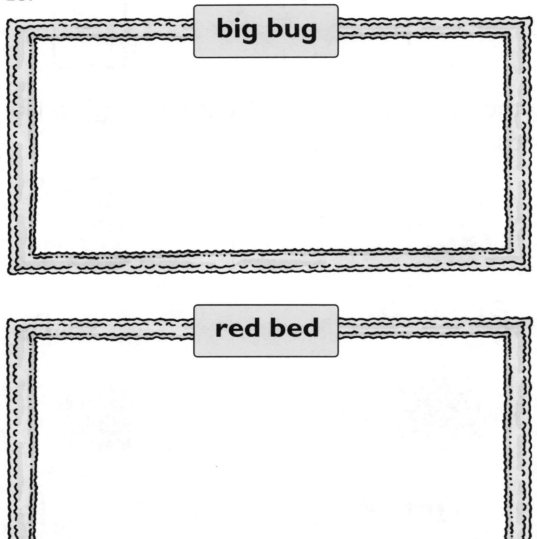

big bug

red bed

Remember to say the sounds clearly, 'buh' not 'bee,' 'ssss' not 'suh,' 'mmm' not 'muh'. It is very important to model the correct sound. If you are unsure, many sites on the Internet are good for listening to the right sounds and incorporating them into fun songs.

Alphabet phonics

● Say the phonics alphabet. Colour each letter a different colour.

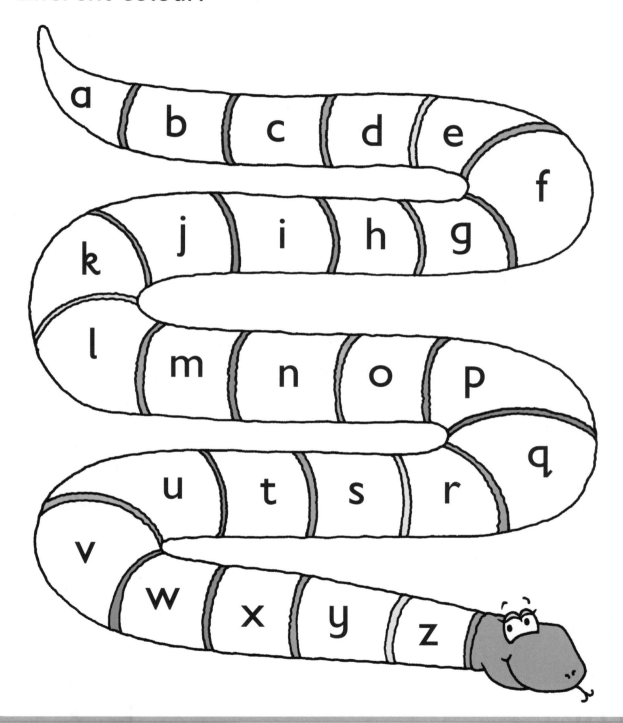

a b c d e f
k j i h g
l m n o p
q u t s r
v w x y z

Well done!
Now colour
the next star.

Word match

● Look at and read these words. Draw a line to match the ones that are the same.

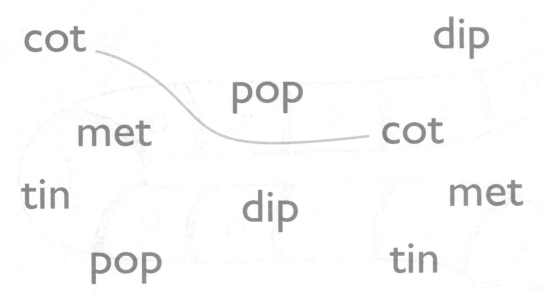

cot   dip

pop   cot

met

tin   met

dip

pop   tin

● Look at and read these words. Copy each word in the space. Draw lines to match the pictures to the words.

mug _ _ _ _

dog _ _ _ _

net _ _ _ _

rat _ _ _ _

Phonic sounds <u>ch</u> and <u>sh</u>

- Look at the pictures and say the words. Write the missing <u>ch</u> letters.

<u>ch</u>

___ ___ ips   ___ ___ ain   ___ ___ in

- Look at the pictures and say the words. Write the missing <u>sh</u> letters.

<u>sh</u>

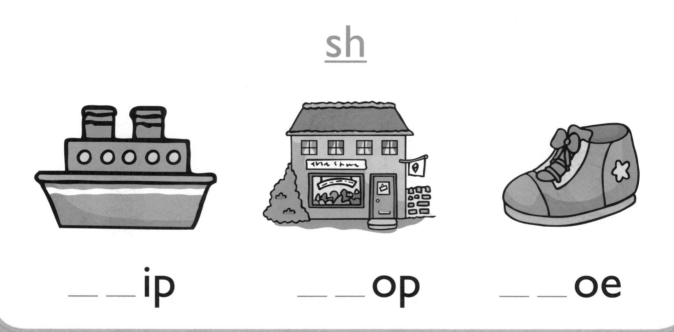

___ ___ ip   ___ ___ op   ___ ___ oe

Well done!
Now colour
the next star.

Phonic sounds <u>th</u> and <u>ng</u>

● Write the missing <u>th</u> letters and say the two words. Colour the <u>th</u>in block blue and the <u>th</u>ick block red.

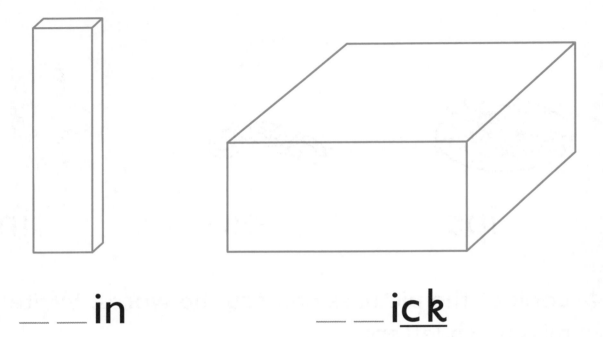

_ _ in

_ _ i<u>ck</u>

● Look at the pictures and say the words. Write the missing <u>ng</u> letters.

ri _ _

swi _ _

ki _ _

Phonic sounds <u>ee</u> and <u>ai</u>

● Say the words for the pictures. Colour the pictures that have the <u>ee</u> sound in the word.

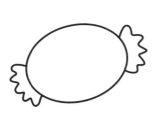  

● Say the words for the pictures. Colour the pictures that have the <u>ai</u> sound in the word.

Which sound?

● Say the word for each picture. Choose the correct sound to finish the word. Write the letters.

<u>sh</u>   <u>ch</u>

fi __ __

<u>ck</u>   <u>ng</u>

ri __ __

<u>sh</u>   <u>ck</u>

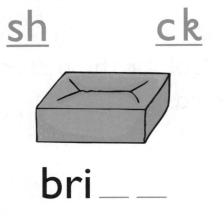

bri __ __

<u>ee</u>   <u>zz</u>

<u>sh</u> __ __ p

<u>ll</u>   <u>ee</u>

do __ __

<u>th</u>   <u>ai</u>

<u>ch</u> __ __ r

Make a sound collection by gathering toys/objects that start with the same phonemes (letter sound), for example 'b': a toy bus, ball, bat, book, balloon and boat. See how many different collections of phonetic sound piles you can make.

Reading sentences

Read these phrases. Draw a line to match each phrase to the right picture.

cat on a red mat

dog on a bed

doll in a cot

bus on a ro<u>ck</u>

Well done!
Now colour
the next star.

Collins Easy Learning
Certificate of Achievement

Well Done!

This certificate is awarded to ....

for successfully completing ....

Age .... Date ....

Signed ....

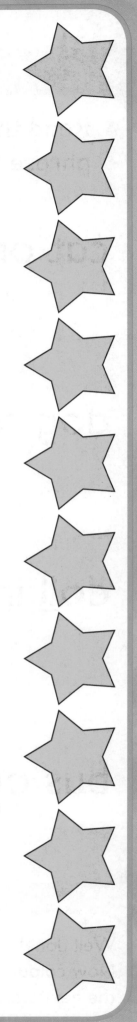